DIGITAL DECLUTTER

DIGITAL DECLUTTER

SLOANE MONTGOMERY

CONTENTS

CHAPTER 1

Introduction to Digital Clutter and its Impact

The development of technology that changes as quickly as digital technology creates a challenging context for those of us who use electronic tools. On the one hand, computer, internet, and device-based tools make our personal and professional lives easier in countless ways. On the other hand, they contribute to a state of fragmented attention, constant distractions, and information overload - all side effects of digital life that cumulatively could be described as digital clutter. This digital clutter requires everyone who uses these tools to think critically and intentionally about how we structure our use of them so that we engage with meaningful content, work effectively and efficiently, and find time for mental consolidation, relaxation, and reflection away from the screen.

The social and commercial push toward constant connectivity has created a state of interruption upon which we have been slow to adapt. Multitasking and other strategies for handling this constant deluge of stimuli, such as continuous partial attention, take a heavy toll both in terms of cognitive function and emotional peace. By making small and deliberate changes to how we interact with electronic tools, we can reclaim a greater degree of focus and sanity. This book is designed to turn these insights into actions and habits that allow us to enjoy the benefits of digital technology without feeling like we sold our soul. Turn the page.

Defining Digital Clutter

Over the last decade, a large portion of the world has fallen into an uncontrolled hypnotic trance, captivated by blue screens and beams of light. While the term "digital clutter" may seem like a form of lighthearted technological jargon, the influence of our growing digital clutter exceeds far beyond the workplace. Whether it's people taking an excessive number of photos without actually enjoying the precious moments or a slew of employees relishing in the satisfaction of their quick responsive "email" cyber badges, the distractions of digital clutter now pose an unparalleled threat to our ability to truly be in live, present, and focused. Just as the real-world stronghold of clutter and an overwhelming sense of disorganization can act as an obstacle to achieving our physical goals, the increasing grip of digital clutter has the power to block our ability of liberation, relief, and healing that is packed with a wealth of mental, emotional, and spiritual benefits. Regardless of the astounding benefits of living in the digital age, we must work diligently to make sure the wondrous technology of this time works for us.

CHAPTER 2

Understanding the Psychological Effects of Screen

It seems trite now to suggest that digital products, particularly social media, are designed to pull us in, keep us coming back, and keep us looking at screens. They are developed to rid us of time, to keep our brains in a dopamine-rich instant-reward cycle, and to show us only carefully crafted pictures of other people's happy lives, rich lives, loved lives – the lives they want to display, not their true life. This is fundamental. Unfortunately, discussing these claims often sounds like the modern version of 'keep children away from the computer if you don't want their brains liquifying into a putrefied mush and running out of their ears', and is therefore generally disregarded by the people who need to start seriously thinking about it. Furthermore, many people treat their phones and other screen-embedded gadgets the same way they perceive their own skin – part of their bodies, integral to their existence, the first thing they lay a hand to in the dark. Turning them off for even a few minutes feels like death, so it's only natural that they avoid doing anything to question the logic of their troubleshooting actions, making their reliance harder to break.

Cognitive Overload and Decision Fatigue

Cognitive Overload is a research term used to describe the situation in which the user of a digital device (such as a smartphone or tablet) has a mismatch of the demands of using the device compared to their cognitive abilities to manipulate or garner information from the device. Digital devices are known to be prone to giving users health issues resulting from prolonged or intense usage. When subjected to this excessive use, the brain is forced to juggle with an immense amount of rapid switching tasks, compared to what it is fully capable of handling. According to the American Psychological Association, the brain is not designed to pay attention to more than one thing at a time. Therefore, when bombarded with a constant spill of incoming information, such as the inflowing tidbits of knowledge which are common in daily digital life, the brain becomes saturated with too much information leading to what is known as digital cognitive overload. The brain specializes in performing tasks that have little to no delays when working with digital devices. Digital tasks and our brain necessitate an incoming prompt and quick reaction to the task at hand. Providing consistent feedback on productivity depending on the nature of tasks performed on digital devices is the most effective way to reduce cognitive overload. Devices that limit this feedback reduce productivity and enhance decision fatigue and frustrating technology experiences, leading to a vogue of reduced user capability, known as the dumbing down effect.

Marshall McLuhan, the media guru of the 1960s, famously stated that the "content of every new medium is always an old medium trying to figure out what to do with the new medium." He meant that novel forms of human expression, for example, the television show in the 1960s, come into being by simulating a well-understood, established medium, for instance, the popular radio show of the time. This content, therefore, when initially created in a new medium is nothing new at all and does not represent the potential or the essence of the medium itself. It takes time and exploration for inspiration and invention to produce new and exciting new media content. Thus, for years, TV shows were simply camera recordings of radio programs, a banal way to use the new medium. Ever since McLuhan articulated this concept, scholars have conducted various studies, each stemming from a different discipline, which appear to confirm McLuhan's prediction very strongly. When any new medium emerges, some people will use it to create something exciting and new. We also know from McLuhan's insight that such content will be long in coming.

CHAPTER 3

Strategies for Digital Decluttering

Now that you understand the philosophy underlying digital decluttering, we can move on to more concrete items. In this section, we will present specific techniques designed to facilitate a deep engagement with the digital tools you depend on most. We divide our discussion into several parts: First, we will describe the key principles of digital minimalism - fundamental habits and a philosophy for technology use designed to maximize personal value and minimize the harm to your psychological well-being. Next, we will present a thirty-day minimalist technology detox designed to help digital maximalists face fears they have about disconnection and to illustrate the changes they can expect from adopting the minimalist way for their digital tool use. After this expurgatory process has set the stage and illuminated the direction forward, we will discuss the most successful tactics for a more careful and contemplated reengagement, focused first on reclaiming leisure time, where we will reclaim, or claim for the first time, our leisure hours. Finally, we will help make our world safe for communication technology, describing a balanced approach that minimizes the harm and maximizes the value. With these new habits and philosophical foundations in place, you will find yourself ready to lean into a digital world's benefits while not selling your soul for them.

Setting Priorities and Goals

When we use our fleeting attention to constantly switch between cyberspaces and think with our fingers by typing text, we can prevent the deeper thoughts that result in meaningful living. Other issues to consider include finding your 'good enough' standard, avoiding the Procrastination Doom Loop, mapping out your ideal day, aiming for a more focused to-do list, and building an evening routine that ties up tasks so your brain doesn't have to. Capture all this thinking in something you can add to a digital notebook as you go. Put down a goal and, if you have one, revisit your own value statement to see if it connects. After determining a few of your own values, ask: 'What do I want my life to be about?' All elements of pushing the power button challenge value, create, enable, or build human capital concurrently.

Before you start adding things to your calendar or to-do list, you need to determine what things are truly worth doing - the activities that are connected to your priorities and values. Simple living means doing less of the less important things. The Digital Declutter calendar deliberately creates empty space to schedule in reflection and leisure, two areas essential for deep living.

CHAPTER 4

Mindful Consumption of Digital Content

Since the publication of the first edition of this book in early 2019, the idea of digital minimalism and its urgent call for more care in our relationship to technology have met with a wide-ranging and increasingly sympathetic audience. Thousands of people have adopted this philosophy and many are diligently applying its challenges to their lives. An issue that sometimes comes up among those practicing digital minimalism is the uncomfortable reality that the digital minimalist's advocacy of using technology to serve the things we deeply value often butts heads with the so-called attention economy - the lucrative business model that powers so much of the digital innovations, and social media in particular, that make our smartphone dominated existence increasingly appealing. In this chapter, we discuss this tension and explore a mindset that can guide the digital minimalist in this conflict: mindful consumption of digital content.

Practicing Digital Minimalism

Minimalism is the ongoing process of eliminating nonessential, noninducing activities so that we can focus on that which is truly essential, so we can focus on what truly matters, because of which increases happiness. Because to eliminate our life, we can be in a position to intentionally fill it with practices that allow us to relish life when we discover our perfect fit. The concept of digital minimalism is an important force in helping to eliminate all the junk that tech companies have added to the Internet to attract our attention and keep us dependent. The ethos of digital minimalism is a compelling case for a world in which we support tech that serves us and encourages us to slip back into a highly aware and much less stressful life.

The most important psychological defense we have in the race for attention in a high-tech society is the ability to be comfortable 'missing out'. A major source of stress in modern life is the fact that we suffer from information and activity overload and have forgotten that we have this basic choice; we can choose not to compete. Minimalism is the art of knowing how much is just enough. Beyond that, we can spend time and energy on our real goals. Once we have this mindset, we have the freedom to choose the things that give us the most satisfaction in life, especially our primary purpose. In minimalism, we limit the excess trappings of our excesses and stop giving our time and energy to experiences and activities that we know are non-intriguing, but continue to consume them almost to the level of addiction. By doing this, we remove the confrontation and free up the energy to invest in the things we value.

CHAPTER 5

Creating a Personalized Digital Detox Plan

What behavior has become challenging for you to govern on your own? Is this a permanent limitation, a temporary limitation, or potentially a versatile limitation? How would you like to change this behavior moving forward? How do you see reshaping this limitation in the future? What is it about this media platform that might make you hesitant to give it up? Once you have removed the service for the thirty-day period, how can you reintroduce it? Will it be different? What will be easier to maintain if you keep the service out of this month for a brief period?

Now that you have a firm understanding of the potential benefits of a digital declutter and the strategies to get there, take a moment to create your customized digital detox plan. Simply step through the following questions and jot down your answers on a blank piece of paper. This worksheet will guide you as you craft your own digital decluttering transition, leveraging the strategies described in the previous chapters and adapted to your particular life and situation.

Assessing Current Digital Habits

Truth to my left bump trap I'm no longer preference caveat around human behavior behind me. The digital tools from which this urge harnessed to amplify a last. In these efforts, essential humanity served. The rest within less. With this animation descended by these digital tools it's now time to finally open a window begin the work of learning how to decide what to bring back inside.

As a guiding principle, consider this general observation about digital tools: In a general psychological propensity toward binging, they're more likely to exploit legacy weaknesses than create new ones. It's for this reason that when you consider the specific details of digital technologies and urges, you'll find that digital minimalism ideas often specify ancient activities—primal biologically inherent to the human condition—like you look infamously avoiding. Require learned and popularized. This is because these urges arose independently in different periods scattered millennia and activated to ensure different goals: female poppies flowers, research, but your network binging and charged as general is not all should rules this importantly, to be natural separation, survival, economic favor is not here, nor are the solitude.

In preparation for your own digital declutter, we need to take a long look in the procedural mirror of the smartphone, tablet, and computer habits of the day. To begin this process of assessment, I'm going to ask that you ignore the abstract prose advertising the products from which these habits stem and instead consider what kind of value the technological tools actually provide. This question—that is, what will digital minimalism mean to me?—is, of course, much harder to answer in the most general sense. The activities or people specific to your world that wax to fill your available time with fulfillment and connection can be hard to pin down in the abstract.

CHAPTER 6

Utilizing Technology to Enhance Productivity

Digital minimalist tools cover the dots so that no extra tasks must be completed. For example, the Pura Scents device uses machine learning to analyze what customers like and dislike based on the way they respond to different scents emitted. A complex device with a simple and intuitive interface, the Pura Scents smart air freshener contains a lot of AI. The system is useful without any additional effort and motivates no other tasks. The yield via a single input is maximized. Third-level tools are the best implementation of the ideas of our minimalism and lead to work transfer. The automation might involve machine learning, but as with the Pura Scents, what is important is not how it is done but what is needed. Defining necessary output first ensures that the right AI best practices are followed.

When a physical environment is reduced to only the items needed for our goals, we are able to more easily discern what needs to be done. The final phase of this method of decluttering is called "third-level tools." Monotasking is also believed by proponents of self-help literature. These writers acknowledge that both prioritizing effectively and not overcommitting are important. At famous Boot

Camps for students, for example, trainers now teach productivity-enhancing strategies and urge them to implement these strategies. Although for different reasons, both advocate monotasking and second- and third-level tools. is sometimes criticized for its high-pressure work environment, and priorities are set from the top down. The company does, but, trust its employees to use their third-level tools to innovate and to follow its lead.

Digital Tools for Time Management

- To-Do Lists. This feature is easily accessible on smartphones, despite the temptation to over-inform and cause anxiety by such tools. Create a map: Set work time limits. Reconnect with nature. Record episode length. Program-related to-do items. Set family time limits. Prep quick and healthy work meals. Assign personal project ideas.

- Calendars. After decluttering, certain events might vanish from your life. Once you regularly keep your calendar, a significantly less busy, more focused life might be the result. These apps are helpful during the transition, for the rapid resolution of scheduling disputes, and for travel. When a drawback presents itself to you, assess the validity of the schedule input.

Not all digital tools are bad. In you will apply a process similar to "Everything in Its Place" to your digital world. While these tools will help you maintain digital organization, you should use them less often than paper planners, as extended screen time can lead to mental and physical health issues. For prominent color mapping and sketch options, paper planners and journals containing both lined and blank pages are valuable alternatives for such tasks. Key digital tools include the following:

CHAPTER 7

Balancing Screen Time with Real-World Activities

Model screen balance. The old adage "Do as I say, not as I do" doesn't work in this space. It's important to admit to iPhone addiction and show children, from personal experience, the process of how you are eliminating clutter from your life and/or downgrading depressing activities so you can intentionally use these devices.

Electronic devices don't have to be entertained. Trust that boredom passes. In fact, it is good for them as it exercises their imagination and problem-solving skills. When children are constantly being entertained by screens, they don't get the chance to experience the gift of boredom.

Set daily and weekly limits on recreational screen time. Realize that screen time is a valuable privilege, not an essential right. Children should balance screen time with "golden time" (activities such as playing with siblings, friends, reading, playing with construction toys, drawing, coloring in) and "green time" (outdoor physical play, suitable outdoor chores).

Keeping screen time to a minimum is virtually impossible, and in some cases, undesirable. However, this doesn't mean that what we do in real life should automatically take a back seat to what's happening on the screens. Here are some suggestions to help balance screen time with real life.

Promoting Physical Well-Being
- Take breaks: Brief breaks—just a minute or two long—but frequent are recommended every 200 minutes when working at the computer. Stand up, take a deep breath, stretch your arms, shoulders, neck, and legs, and practice deep focusing. Get involved with your environment even if it is for a minute to prevent eye strain. Keep in mind and watch your computer, TV, video games, and your phone, in that order.

- Use your computer properly: Sit up straight and rest your wrists on a pad in front of the keyboard, with your elbows at your sides and your hands at or slightly below elbow level. Make sure you have enough legroom; raise your feet if necessary. Rest your eyes about 16 inches from the screen for text work and about two feet for print for handwriting, painting, etc. Use a soft glare-free background and use task lighting such as a hovering lamp.

- Aired and not out of date: Computers consume a significant amount of energy. Therefore, they generate heat when they are used. Temperature regulation mechanisms can clog, causing your computer to fry if not attended to.

CHAPTER 8

Maintaining a Sustainable Digital Lifestyle

The smaller your digital empire, the easier it will be to administer, maintain and secure. It will also provide less fodder and negative reaction to the various digital trolls currently plying their trade. The first task in maintaining your new digital life is to focus your energies on the devices and online services that are serving your goals well and discard all the others. Take the tools that you need to achieve your goals and make them the hub of your digital life. The goal is not to have fewer digital tools, but to become more productive with the ones you already use.

The twin goals of maintaining a minimalist habitat that keeps your attention sharp and your commitments meaningful and aligning your digital lifestyle with them are realizing your values. There are two strategies for doing this and they involve mirroring the two main strategies of non-digital decluttering that we have previously discussed. The first is to adopt a Dulcolax lifestyle. The second is to focus on simple, direct and high-quality service relationships and accept the constraints that come with them.

Your newly clutter-free digital life will come under constant pressure from people who do not share your values. The world's most powerful designers and engineers are working hard to ensure that the services that pay their salaries command more and more of your time and resources. They develop sophisticated tools designed to exploit the cognitive habits of the brain's pleasure centers. Slowly but surely, you will find your life is visual clutter all over again.

Establishing Healthy Boundaries

Setting the Digital Rulebook: While many activities related to work, community participation, and personal time may require connectivity, a bit of conscious thinking and rules outlining what is considered healthy screen use may restrict some of the time dedicated to digital distractions. Devices that work for us, instead of being a hindrance, are those that inform us when we need to know something and then leave us alone when we don't. A good plan would be to enforce a one and a half to two-hour major time block during which work is done and emails and messages are checked. After we are done, we should close these tabs and put our devices on silent mode so that we can be immersed in other activities without the expectation that we would keep checking in on a regular basis. The aim is to make better decisions about when we are willing to use digital tools so that they support the intentions we have about our time, our opinions, and the people we are spending precious moments with, instead of what a device wants from us. Fewer impulses result in more focus and dedication to all the moments in our lives.

The first step to engaging in regular digital decluttering is establishing healthy boundaries for technology in our lives. Unlike a physical detox, where we can totally abstain from certain activities like consuming processed sugar, there is no way to remove the need for everyday necessities like responding to emails or chatting with co-workers using various messaging platforms. Instead of a complete removal from technology, we need to define borders that divide the needs from the optional, the essential from the non-essential. The Aegean concept of all things in moderation is crucial here—in these modern times, we need to figure out boundaries in what we consume, especially when it comes to digital distractions. Some questions to ask and a few ideas to establish healthy boundaries include:

CHAPTER 9

The Future of Digital Wellness

Even if science and medicine were to make great new discoveries in brain and mind to mitigate the drawbacks of pervasive digital living, the human race has the potential to overdo it again. The digital world does have some virtues: no one really wants to stop all of human progress in the name of restoring youthful simplicity. The world now has the sort of scientific calculus that can prescribe the right data diet, the right amount of time to look at screens, and the right algorithm diet that balances the social influence of echo chambers versus the enrichment of constant challenging cognitive circumstances. But the fact that many of the discontents of a digital life are easily reversed does not mean that current public health decision makers are eager to limit the flood of digital engagement. Medical knowledge is rarely used to curtail commercial opportunities. But without some brakes or some guidance, as a species, we will certainly find newer and better ways to burn ourselves out mentally, or worse.

Many who study digital decluttering and other mindfulness-based digital wellness strategies are pessimistic about the systemic and comprehensive remedies to be had. There is no single solution, no single policy that will restore the public and private digital landscape to the utopian dream of the 1990s, a time of great hope and hunger for the free flow of information. The internet does not have a singularly clear path back to its original ideal of being a disintermediated, decentralized way to connect and share with others. Adding a foundation for a digital mindfulness discipline, even though it will not fix everything, can at least begin the process of slowing down the digital discontents and stop the spread of new worries for future generations.

Trends in Technology and Well-Being

For individuals, however, desiring not to be disrupted, smart machines also provide continuous health monitoring and early diagnosis support tools that promise benefits in terms of increased safety and reduced cost.

Such dispersion of technology has the potential to plug poor and remote villages into urban economic networks, just as historical inventions like highways, railroads, and telephone networks did. Smart machines, when exploited effectively, have the potential to provide the luxury of leisure, harnessing technology to utilize our investment in capital and automation to produce better societies collectively. Companies like Google work passionately to solve grand challenges of our time using information technologies: they produce driverless cars, develop renewable energy options, disrupt the utility industry, and even develop machine learning designed to overcome human biases.

For example, consider our work lives. In the workplace, productivity-enhancing technologies are providing countless benefits. These tools plug workers into global networks, allowing them to share knowledge, build relationships, and understand remote sites. This is true even for workers placed into various forms of digital bondage. Our earlier case study of Bangladeshi garment workers showed that many workers perceived that they received higher wages after they started using mobile phones.

At the frontier of work on the effects of technological change, many researchers identify potential virtues of information and communication technologies (ICTs) for well-being. While our review will later focus on some potential negative consequences of our digital age, we should underscore that technology can make truly meaningful and tangible improvements to human well-being, safety, and liberation across a wide range of domains.

CHAPTER 10

Conclusion: Embracing a Balanced Digital Existence

In fact, minimalism is much more than just a set of strategies for being clutter-free with your technology and is proud of living simply. In the digital domain, minimalism at its core reveals a profoundly more beautiful way to engage with the tools that have come to dominate our lives. The minimalist philosophy of technology use alone isn't opposed to innovation or hand-waving at the idea of moderation. Its purpose is to provide an empowering set of ideas for thriving in a high-tech world. Digital minimalism is a very accessible and 21st-century application of the broader minimalist core principle of prioritizing life activities that we care about the most over activities that bring us the most immediate pleasure.

Digital Clutter offers many strategies for taking back control over our digital lives, but the goal of this book isn't to establish a back-to-nature vision for existence in a digital age. After all, digital improvements introduced over the past two decades have been genuinely transformative to the betterment of individuals' personal and professional lives. As we explored in the previous chapter, new technologies can enable us to live lives that are highly productive and deeply enjoyable. This is why the decision to embrace digital minimalism is not an ultimate philosophy for a simpler life, but instead a foundational strategy to live a better life.

enjoyable. This is why the decision to embrace digital minimalism is not an ultimate philosophy for a simpler life, but instead a foundational strategy to live a better life.